DIG DEEP INTO FOSSILS

Digging Up Human Fossils

BY CHARLOTTE TAYLOR

Enslow PUBLISHING

INVESTIGATE!

Please visit our website, www.enslow.com. For a free color catalog of all our high-quality books, call toll free 1-800-398-2504 or fax 1-877-980-4454.

Library of Congress Cataloging-in-Publication Data

Names: Taylor, Charlotte, 1978- author.
Title: Digging up human fossils / Charlotte Taylor.
Description: New York : Enslow Publishing, [2022] | Series: Dig deep into fossils | Includes index.
Identifiers: LCCN 2020014227 | ISBN 9781978521568 (library binding) | ISBN 9781978521544 (paperback) | ISBN 9781978521551 (set) | ISBN 9781978521575 (ebook)
Subjects: LCSH: Fossil hominids–Juvenile literature. | Paleoanthropology–Juvenile literature.
Classification: LCC GN282 .T39 2022 | DDC 569.9–dc23
LC record available at https://lccn.loc.gov/2020014227

Published in 2022 by
Enslow Publishing
101 West 23rd Street, Suite #240
New York, NY 10011

Designer: Katelyn E. Reynolds
Editor: Megan Quick

Photo credits: Cover, pp. 1 (skull) bazzier/Shutterstock.com; cover, pp. 1–24 (background) Click Bestsellers/Shutterstock.com; cover, pp. 1–24 (tools) Serz_72/Shutterstock.com; cover, pp. 1–24 (burst) Foxys Graphic/Shutterstock.com; p. 4 Ivan Mattioli/ iStock / Getty Images Plus; p. 5 Ирина Мещерякова/ iStock / Getty Images Plus; p. 6 Dorling Kindersley/Getty Images; p. 7 Patrick Aventurier/Getty Images; p. 8 Foto24/Gallo Images via Getty Images; p. 8 STEFAN HEUNIS/AFP via Getty Images; p. 9 Irfan Khan/Los Angeles Times via Getty Images; p. 10 dimarik/ iStock / Getty Images Plus; p. 11 Yuji Ohsugi/WireImage/Getty Images; pp. 12, 19, 28 DEA PICTURE LIBRARY/De Agostini via Getty Images; pp. 13, 23 Encyclopaedia Britannica/UIG Via Getty Images; p. 14 Chip HIRES/Gamma-Rapho via Getty Images; p. 15 Agoes Rudianto/Anadolu Agency/Getty Images; p. 15 Creativemarc/ iStock / Getty Images Plus; p. 16 MUJAHID SAFODIEN/AFP via Getty Images; p. 17 Usagi-D/ iStock / Getty Images Plus; p. 17 PTZ Pictures/Shutterstock.com; p. 18 LILLIAN OMARIBA/AFP via Getty Images; p. 20 All the rights for presented photos are my own./ iStock / Getty Images Plus; p. 21 sruilk/Shutterstock.com; p. 22 kwanchaichaiudom/ iStock / Getty Images Plus; p. 25 STEPHANE DE SAKUTIN/AFP via Getty Images; pp. 26, 2 Dave Einsel/Getty Images; p. 29 NOEL CELIS/AFP via Getty Images.

Portions of this work were originally authored by Kathleen Connors and published as *Human Fossils*. All new material in this edition authored by Charlotte Taylor.

Printed in the United States of America

CPSIA compliance information: Batch #CSENS22: For further information contact Enslow Publishing, New York, New York, at 1-800-398-2504.

CONTENTS

WORDS IN THE GLOSSARY APPEAR IN **BOLD** TYPE THE FIRST TIME THEY ARE USED IN THE TEXT.

DIGGING FOR ANSWERS

Does digging up the bones of ancient humans sound spooky? Maybe. But it's an important way of finding out how modern humans—like you!—got here. And that's just what paleoanthropologists do. These scientists can figure out how early humans walked, what they ate, and even how smart they were—all thanks to fossils.

Explore More!

IN THE MID-1800S, ENGLISH SCIENTIST CHARLES DARWIN BECAME ONE OF THE FIRST TO SAY THAT HUMANS AND APES CAME FROM THE SAME **ANCESTOR**.

CHARLES DARWIN

DIGGING UP FOSSILS IS SLOW WORK. THEN IT CAN TAKE YEARS TO PUT THEM TOGETHER AND FIGURE OUT THEIR HISTORY.

Fossils are what is left behind when something dies. They can come from a plant or an animal. They may take thousands or even millions of years to form. Fossils help scientists piece together the puzzle of human **evolution**.

HOW A FOSSIL FORMS

When a plant or animal dies, the soft parts break down. Hard parts like bone and teeth are left behind. Sometimes, these **remains** become buried in sediment, which is bits of stones, sand, shells, or mud from rivers and oceans. Sediment builds up in layers and can harden into rock.

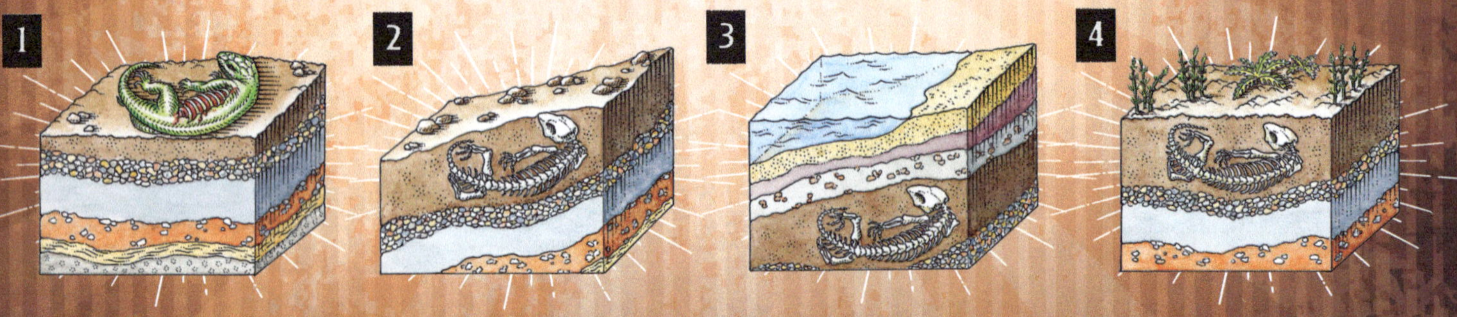

A DEAD ANIMAL IS COVERED IN SEDIMENT, WHICH PRESSES DOWN ON THE REMAINS. THEY SLOWLY TURN TO ROCK AND BECOME A FOSSIL.

Over time, water from the ground works its way into the bones that are buried under sediment. **Minerals** from the water fill tiny open spaces in the bones. Slowly, the minerals replace the bone. The minerals harden and become rock. Now the remains are a fossil.

SCIENTISTS CHIP AWAY AT ROCK TO FIND THE FOSSILS THAT HAVE FORMED UNDERNEATH.

KINDS OF FOSSILS

There are two main kinds of human fossils: body and trace. As you might guess, body fossils come from the body itself. They are almost always the hard parts of the body, such as bones and teeth. Body fossils are the most common kind of fossil.

THESE BODY FOSSILS FOUND IN SOUTH AFRICA INCLUDE PIECES OF BONE AND SOME TEETH.

Explore More!

SOME FOSSILS ARE SO TINY THAT YOU CAN'T SEE THEM WITHOUT A MICROSCOPE. THESE ARE CALLED MICROFOSSILS.

Scientists can tell a great deal from just one body fossil. One leg bone might show how large a person was. A tooth could show what kind of food a person ate. Scientists can compare body fossils to today's humans to see how they are the same or different.

Trace fossils are records of how ancient humans lived. They may include footprints, tooth marks, or even poop! Anything that humans left behind can give us clues about how they lived.

Footprints are a very useful kind of trace fossil. From one footprint fossil, a scientist can answer many questions. How heavy was the human? How tall was he? How did he walk? What was the ground like in that area? If other footprints or fossils are nearby, the scientist can figure out how they were all connected.

THESE FOOTPRINTS BELONG TO AN EARLY HUMAN.

Explore More!

THE OLDEST FOOTPRINT FOSSIL OF A HUMAN ANCESTOR WAS FOUND IN THE AFRICAN COUNTRY OF KENYA. SCIENTISTS BELIEVE THE FOOTPRINT IS ABOUT 1.5 MILLION YEARS OLD!

THE FIRST FOSSILS

When people first started finding early human fossils, they weren't sure what they were. In 1856, part of a **skull** was found in Germany. It was very thick. Scientists didn't know how old it was or if it was even human! They finally figured out the fossil was from a group of very early humans, which they named Neanderthals (*Homo neanderthalensis*).

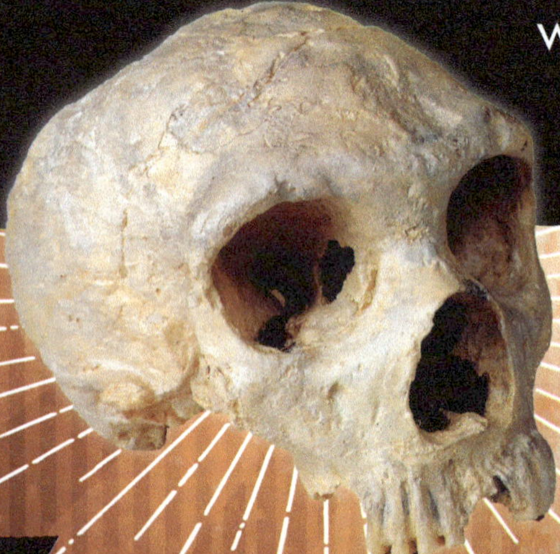

THIS NEANDERTHAL SKULL WAS DISCOVERED IN 1848, BEFORE SCIENTISTS HAD A NAME FOR THE **SPECIES**.

More fossil discoveries show that Neanderthals appeared on Earth at least 200,000 years ago. Modern humans took over about 24,000 to 35,000 years ago.

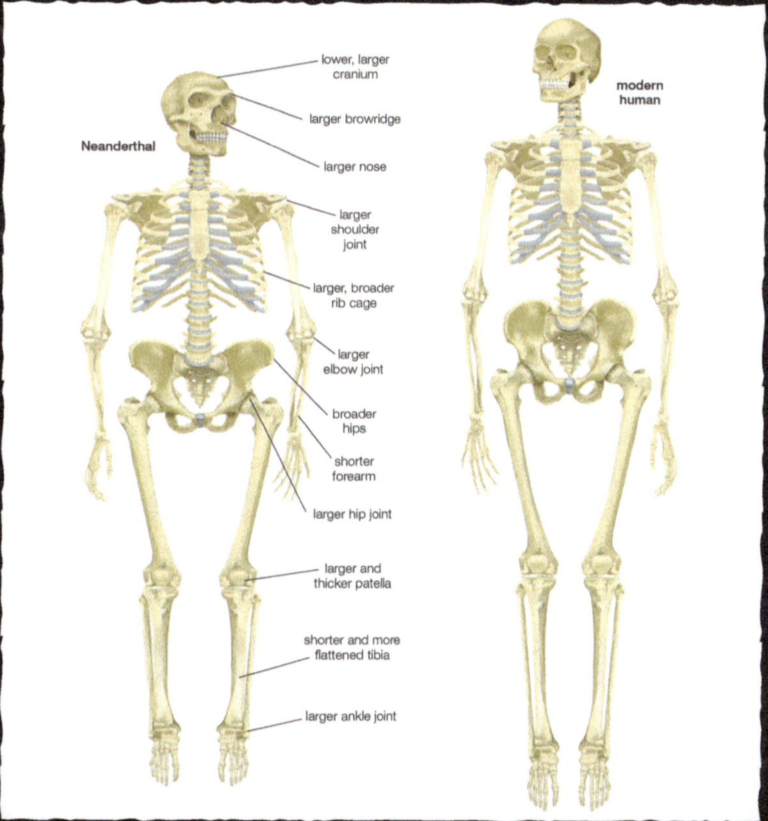

COMPARE THE NEANDERTHAL **SKELETON** (LEFT) TO A MODERN HUMAN SKELETON.

Explore More!

NEANDERTHALS WERE MODERN HUMANS' CLOSEST **RELATIVES.** THEY DIED OUT THOUSANDS OF YEARS AGO, BUT SOME MODERN HUMANS STILL HAVE A BIT OF NEANDERTHAL IN THEM!

CONNECTING HUMANS

In 1891, Eugene Dubois dug up the first fossils of another human species in Indonesia. It was called *Homo erectus*. The species first appeared almost 2 million years ago and disappeared about 200,000 years ago. Since the discovery of *Homo erectus*, scientists have found 20 different human species.

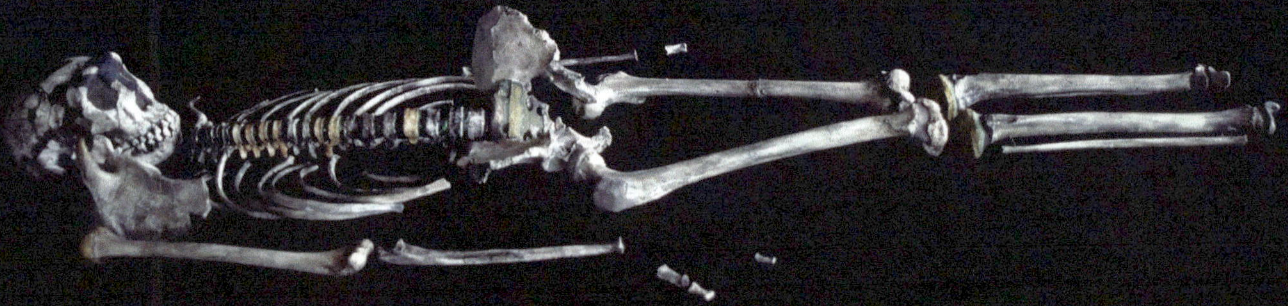

FOSSILS OF EARLY HUMANS LIKE *HOMO ERECTUS* HELP US LEARN WHAT OUR ANCESTORS MAY HAVE LOOKED LIKE.

Explore More!

SCIENTISTS BELIEVE THAT *HOMO ERECTUS* WAS THE FIRST HUMAN SPECIES TO USE OR CONTROL FIRE, ABOUT ONE MILLION YEARS AGO.

Modern humans are part of the species *Homo sapiens.* We are the only human species still alive today. But there was a time when several human species lived on Earth at the same time. Fossils show us that the human family tree has many branches!

THIS FOSSIL OF *HOMO ERECTUS* WAS DISCOVERED IN INDONESIA.

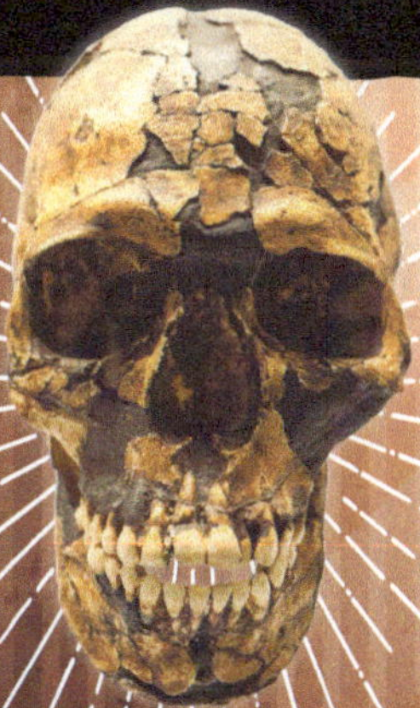

HOMO SAPIENS

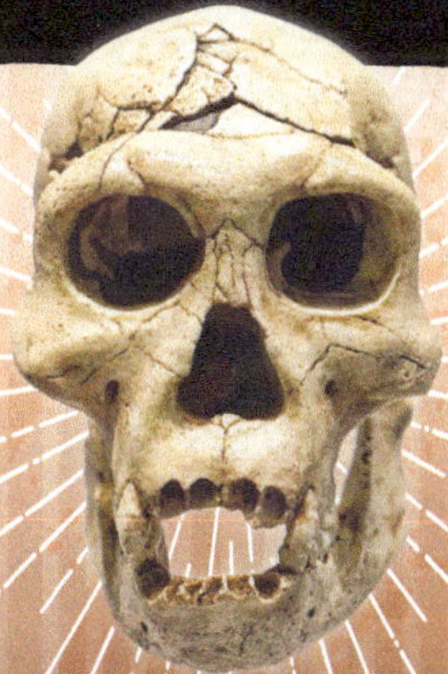

HOMO ERECTUS

APES IN THE FAMILY

We know that humans and apes have a special connection. They're both part of the animal family called Hominidae. Members of this family are called hominids. Ancient hominid fossils show some human features and some ape features. But scientists don't always agree about the connection between these fossils, modern humans, and apes.

THIS FOSSIL, NAMED LITTLE FOOT, HAS BOTH HUMAN AND APE FEATURES.

Explore More!

SCIENTISTS BELIEVE THAT THE COMMON ANCESTOR OF HUMANS AND APES LIVED BETWEEN 6 MILLION AND 8 MILLION YEARS AGO.

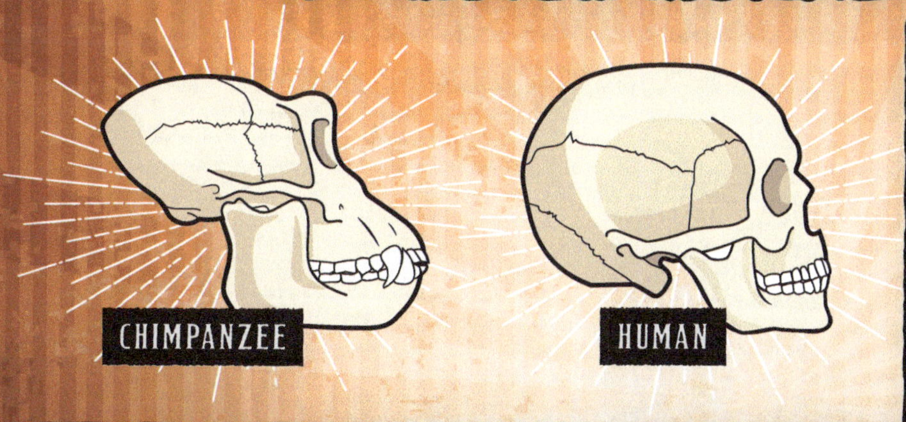

THIS *AUSTRALOPITHECUS* FOSSIL IS OVER 3.5 MILLION YEARS OLD. SCIENTISTS STUDY EARLY HOMINID FOSSILS TO LEARN THE LINK BETWEEN APES AND HUMANS.

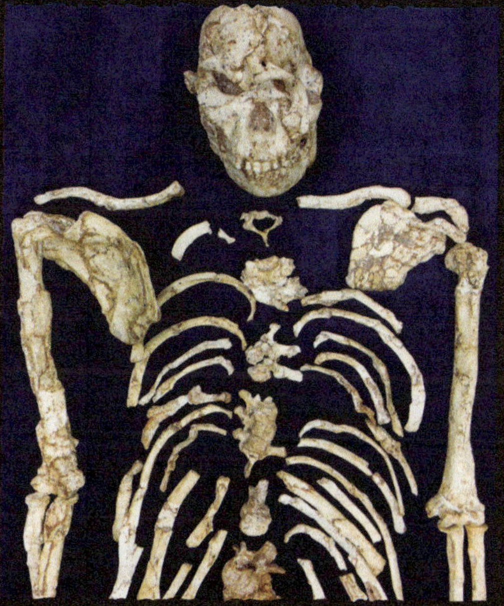

Among all of the apes, chimpanzees and bonobos are most closely related to humans. Scientists study fossils to learn how the common ancestor for chimps, bonobos, and humans ended up **evolving** in such different ways.

HOW OLD IS IT?

Once a fossil is found, paleoanthropologists must try to figure out how old it is. In order to do this, they may use **superposition**. With this method, the scientists find the fossil's age based on the rock layer in which it's found. Another method is radiometric dating. This looks at tiny pieces inside the fossil to see how old it is.

HUMAN SKULLS HAVE CHANGED IN SHAPE AND SIZE OVER THE YEARS.

The oldest fossils of human ancestors date back about 4 million to 6 million years. Many of the oldest of these fossils were found in Africa, where early humans first lived.

EVOLUTION OF THE HOMINID

Explore More!

THE OLDEST KNOWN FOSSILS OF MODERN HUMANS WERE FOUND IN A CAVE IN MOROCCO. SCIENTISTS BELIEVE THAT THEY ARE AROUND 300,000 YEARS OLD.

LEARNING FROM FOSSILS

What can fossils tell us about humans and their ancestors? Fossilized bones offer clues about everything from how they lived to what they ate. For example, studying leg bones helps scientists figure out if our human ancestors spent more time in trees or on the ground.

ANCIENT HUMAN REMAINS LIKE THESE TELL US HOW EARLY PEOPLE LIVED.

Explore More!

PALEOANTHROPOLOGISTS STUDY ANIMAL BONES FOUND NEAR HUMAN FOSSILS. IF THE ANIMAL BONES HAVE MARKS FROM TOOLS, THEY KNOW THE HUMANS CUT UP THE ANIMALS TO EAT.

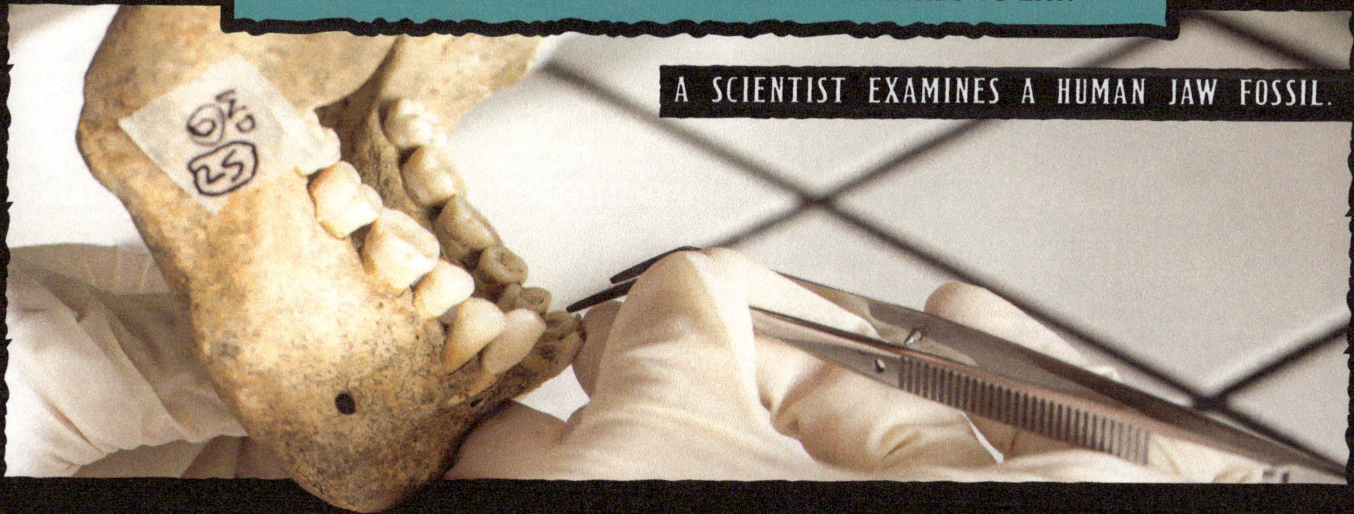
A SCIENTIST EXAMINES A HUMAN JAW FOSSIL.

Fossils of teeth tell us about eating habits. Scientists may study marks left on teeth from food. This will tell them what was eaten in the days before death, such as grasses, fruits, or animals. And the size of skull fossils shows us that the human brain grew as the world became more advanced.

WALKING TALL

Some hominids probably walked on two feet as early as 6 million years ago. But like their ape relatives, they also used their hands and feet to climb trees. The shape of a fossilized leg, hand, or pelvis—a large bone that connects the lower back and hips—shows scientists how early humans moved around.

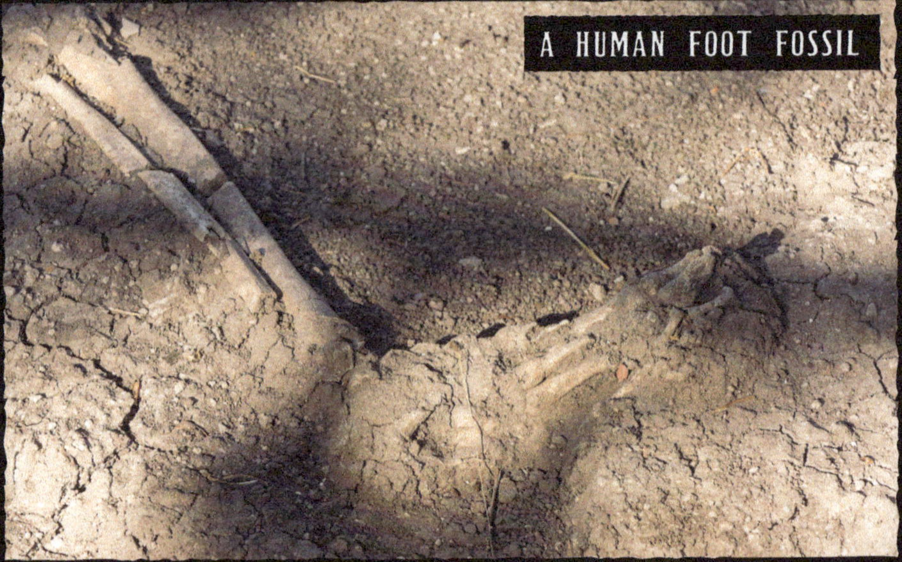

A HUMAN FOOT FOSSIL

Over time, changes in leg and hip bones tell us hominids were walking more and climbing less. Fossils of *Homo erectus* show that our human ancestors could cover lots of ground. This helped in the wide-open grasslands of Africa.

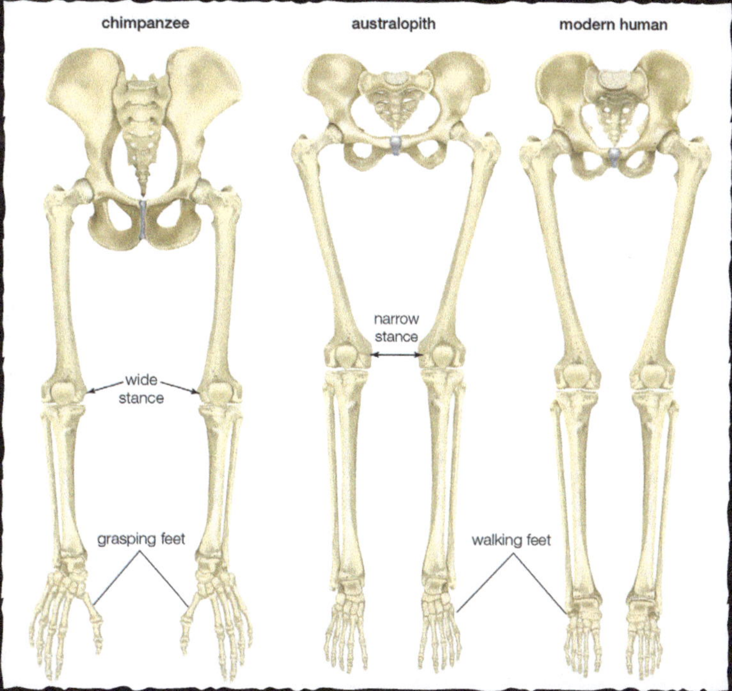

THESE DRAWINGS SHOW THE DIFFERENCE BETWEEN THE LOWER BODY OF THE CHIMP, AN EARLY HUMAN ANCESTOR, AND THE MODERN HUMAN. NOTICE THE CHANGES IN SHAPE.

Explore More!

THE ABILITY TO WALK ON TWO FEET IS ONE MAJOR DIFFERENCE BETWEEN HUMANS AND CHIMPANZEES. THE CHIMP'S SKELETON IS NOT MADE FOR WALKING ON TWO FEET REGULARLY.

DAILY LIFE

Human fossils provide clues about how our ancestors lived from day to day. We know that *Homo erectus* used fire and made simple tools. Because of fossils, we also know that they cared for their sick and older family members.

Neanderthals were much more advanced than *Homo erectus*. They used better tools and they wore clothing. Another thing that paleoanthropologists have learned from fossils is that Neanderthals buried their dead and sometimes marked their graves. We see how, over many thousands of years, humans slowly changed into who they are today.

A MUSEUM IN FRANCE DISPLAYS TOOLS THAT WERE MADE BY NEANDERTHALS.

Explore More!

SCIENTISTS STUDY BONE FOSSILS TO UNDERSTAND HOW CHILDREN FROM OTHER HUMAN SPECIES GREW INTO ADULTS.

FOSSIL ROCK STARS

Over the years, paleoanthropologists have made some very cool fossil discoveries. Some of these finds have been very exciting. In 1974, a 3.2-million-year-old fossilized skeleton was found in Ethiopia. Scientists named it "Lucy." At the time, Lucy was the oldest and most complete skeleton of a human ancestor ever found.

A MODEL OF WHAT LUCY MAY HAVE LOOKED LIKE

"Ardi" was found in Africa in 1992. In 2009, scientists first presented the 4.4-million-year-old skeleton. The fossilized skeleton of a **primate** called "Ida" was also presented in 2009. It taught scientists more about the connection between humans and apes.

LUCY'S SKELETON

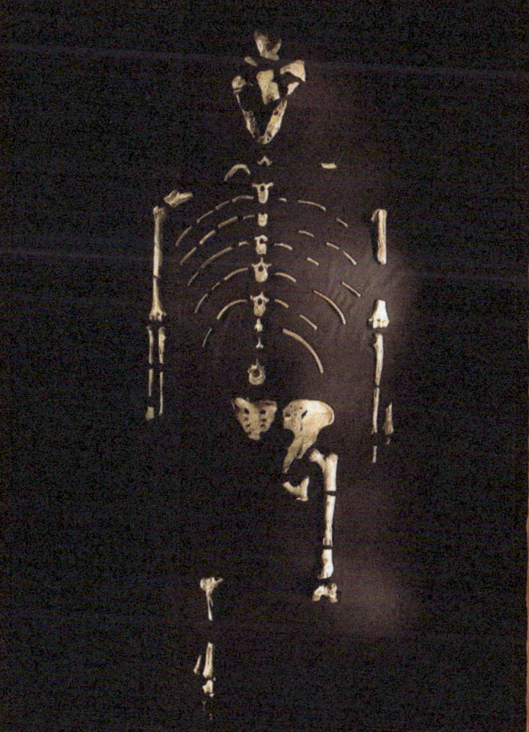

SCIENTISTS FIGURE THAT LUCY WAS AROUND 3 FEET, 7 INCHES TALL (109 CM) AND WEIGHED ABOUT 60 POUNDS (27 KG).

Explore More!

LUCY'S NAME CAME FROM A BEATLES SONG CALLED "LUCY IN THE SKY WITH DIAMONDS." THE SCIENTISTS WHO MADE THE DISCOVERY LISTENED TO THE SONG AFTER THEY FOUND THE FOSSILS.

DISCOVERING THE PAST

New and exciting discoveries of human fossils are being made every year. In 2018, scientists announced they had found a jawbone in Israel that was around 180,000 years old. This means that humans may have moved from Africa 50,000 years earlier than first thought. And in 2019, a study reported the discovery of a new "cousin" of *Homo sapiens* found in the Philippines. This added yet another branch to the human family tree.

IN 2019, A SCIENTIST IN THE PHILIPPINES TALKED ABOUT TOOTH FOSSILS OF A NEW *HOMO SAPIENS* RELATIVE.

Explore More!

SCIENTISTS HAVE FOUND MORE THAN 6,000 FOSSILS FROM HUMANS AND HUMAN ANCESTORS.

Digging up and studying fossils is slow, hard work. But with each new find, scientists learn more about humans' journey through time.

GLOSSARY

ancestor An animal that lived before others in its family tree.

evolution The changes in a living thing that take place over many lifetimes.

evolve To slowly change over a long period of time.

microscope A tool used to view very small objects so they can be seen much larger and more clearly.

mineral Matter found in nature that is not living.

primate Any animal from the group that includes humans, apes, and monkeys.

relative A family member.

remains Parts of a living thing that are left behind after it dies.

skeleton The bony frame of the body.

skull The bony frame of the head and face.

species A group of animals that are all of the same kind.

superposition The placement of layers of rock on top of one another. The lower layers are older than the higher layers.

For More Information

BOOKS

Alkire, Jessie. *Discovering Fossils*. Minneapolis, MN: Abdo Publishing, 2019.

Bright, Michael. *When We Became Humans: Our Incredible Evolutionary Journey*. Lake Forest, CA: Quarto Publishing, 2019.

Oxlade, Chris. *Fossils*. New York, NY: Kingfisher, 2018.

WEBSITES

DK Find Out: Fossil Facts for Kids
www.dkfindout.com/us/dinosaurs-and-prehistoric-life/fossils/
Find out more about fossils, where they're found, and how they're formed.

Ducksters: Fossils
www.ducksters.com/science/earth_science/fossils.php
Discover more fun facts about fossils, then check your knowledge with a quiz.

Human Evolution: You Try It
www.pbs.org/wgbh/aso/tryit/evolution/#
Read more about human evolution, then follow up with a fun activity.

INDEX